TIBETAN
DESIGNS
COLORING BOOK

Marty Noble

DOVER PUBLICATIONS, INC.
Mineola, New York

Introduction

The varied designs created and adapted for this collection are based on Tibetan tankas, mandalas painted in formats other than the tanka, and other Buddhist religious art. Included is art that reflects the influence of traditional Central Asian and Chinese painters. More than half of the designs are based on tankas, Tibetan scroll paintings or drawings usually created on stretched and treated cotton, linen, or muslin that has been polished to a smooth, glossy surface. This form of religious art has roots in Indian cloth painting, in mandalas (symbolic representations of the universe, which were drawn on the ground before portable art forms were developed), and in the scrolls used by storytellers. In addition to variants on the primary colors (such as red, carmine vermilion, arsenic yellow, lapis-lazuli blue, and indigo), the colors most frequently used in tankas are lime white, vitriol green, and gold.

In addition to several images of the Buddha and various depictions of lamas, saints, and great teachers, this group of designs includes Tibetan astrological symbols, the Golden Wheel, ritual bells, green and white Taras, and a myriad of other traditional Tibetan motifs. Lions, elephants, bulls, horses, birds, and more fanciful creatures are shown in profusion. Seven centuries of Tibetan religious art are represented.

Copyright

Copyright © 2002, 2013 by Dover Publications, Inc.
All rights reserved.

Bibliographical Note

Tibetan Designs Coloring Book, published by Dover Publications, Inc., in 2013, is a republication of the edition originally published by Dover in 2002. One additional plate has been added for the present edition.

International Standard Book Number

ISBN-13: 978-0-486-49449-4
ISBN-10: 0-486-49449-7

Manufactured in the United States by RR Donnelley
49449704   2015
www.doverpublications.com

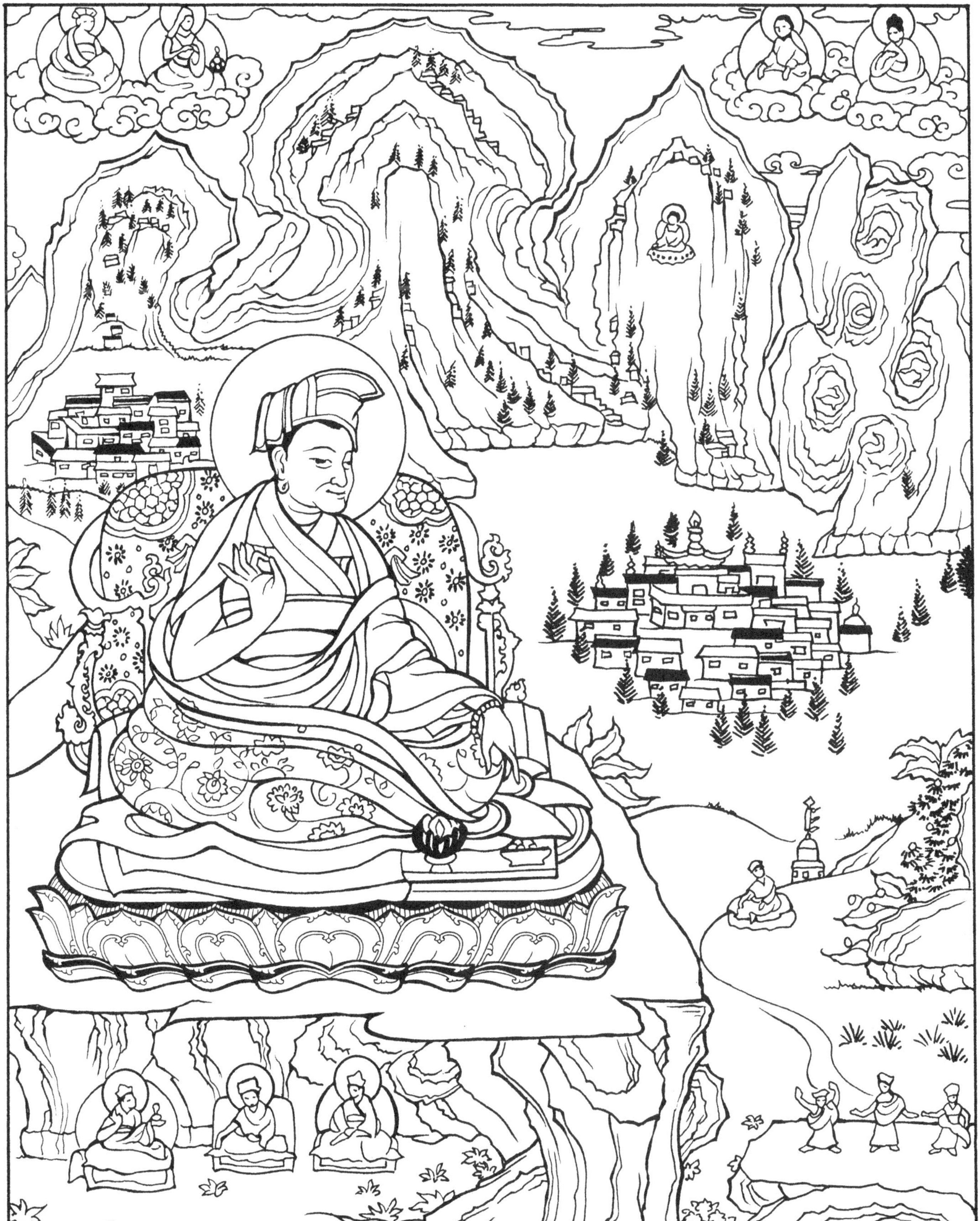

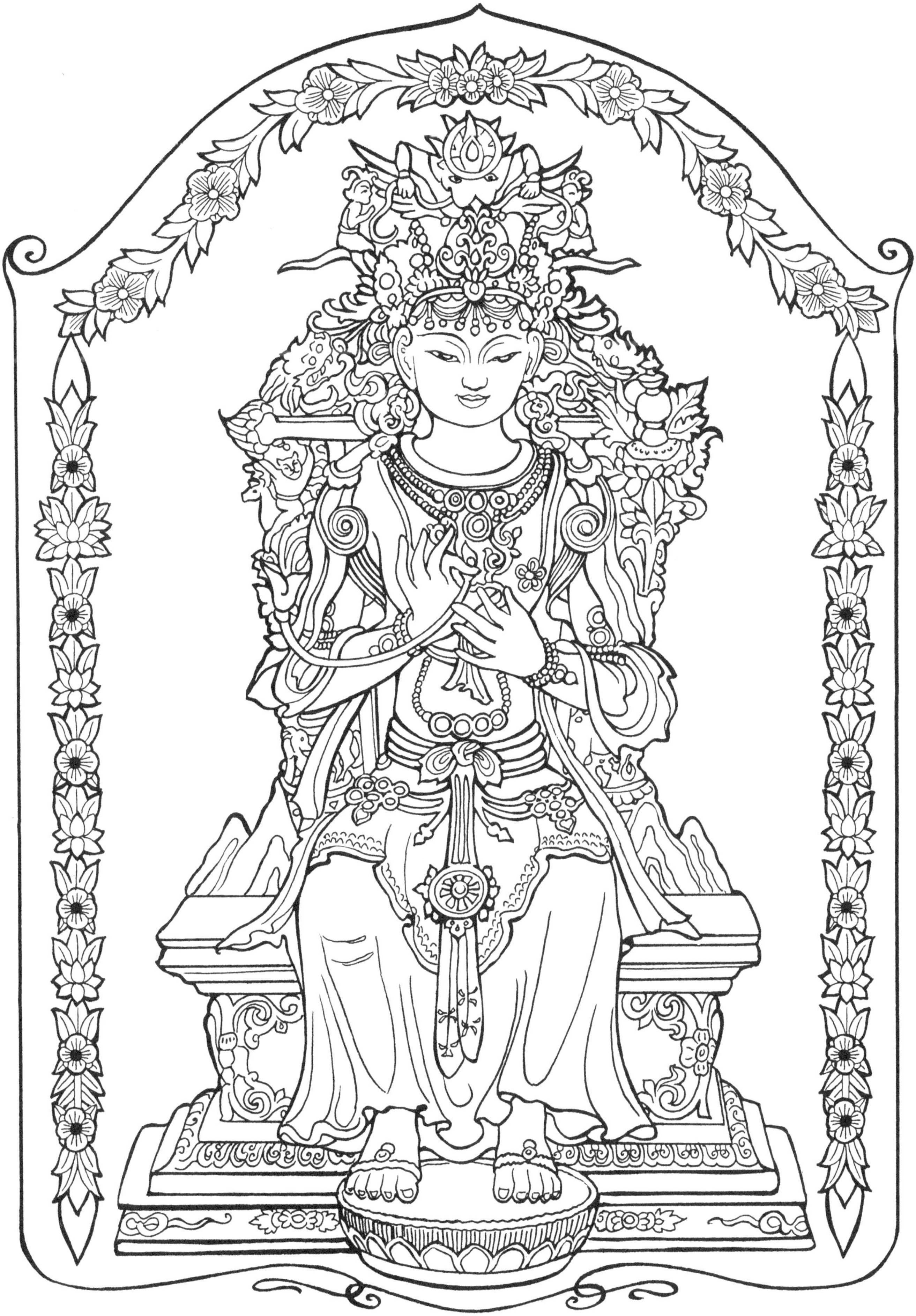

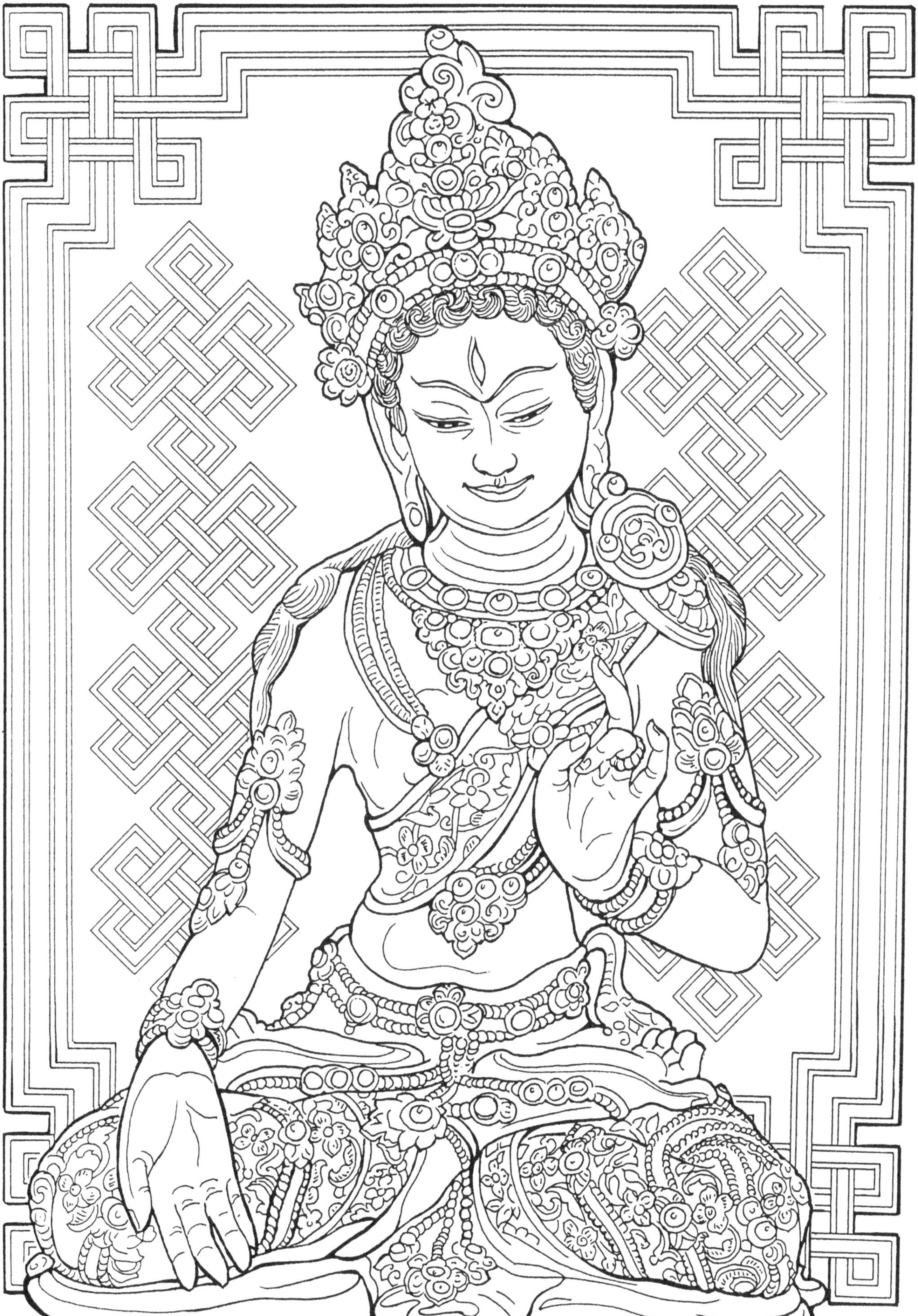

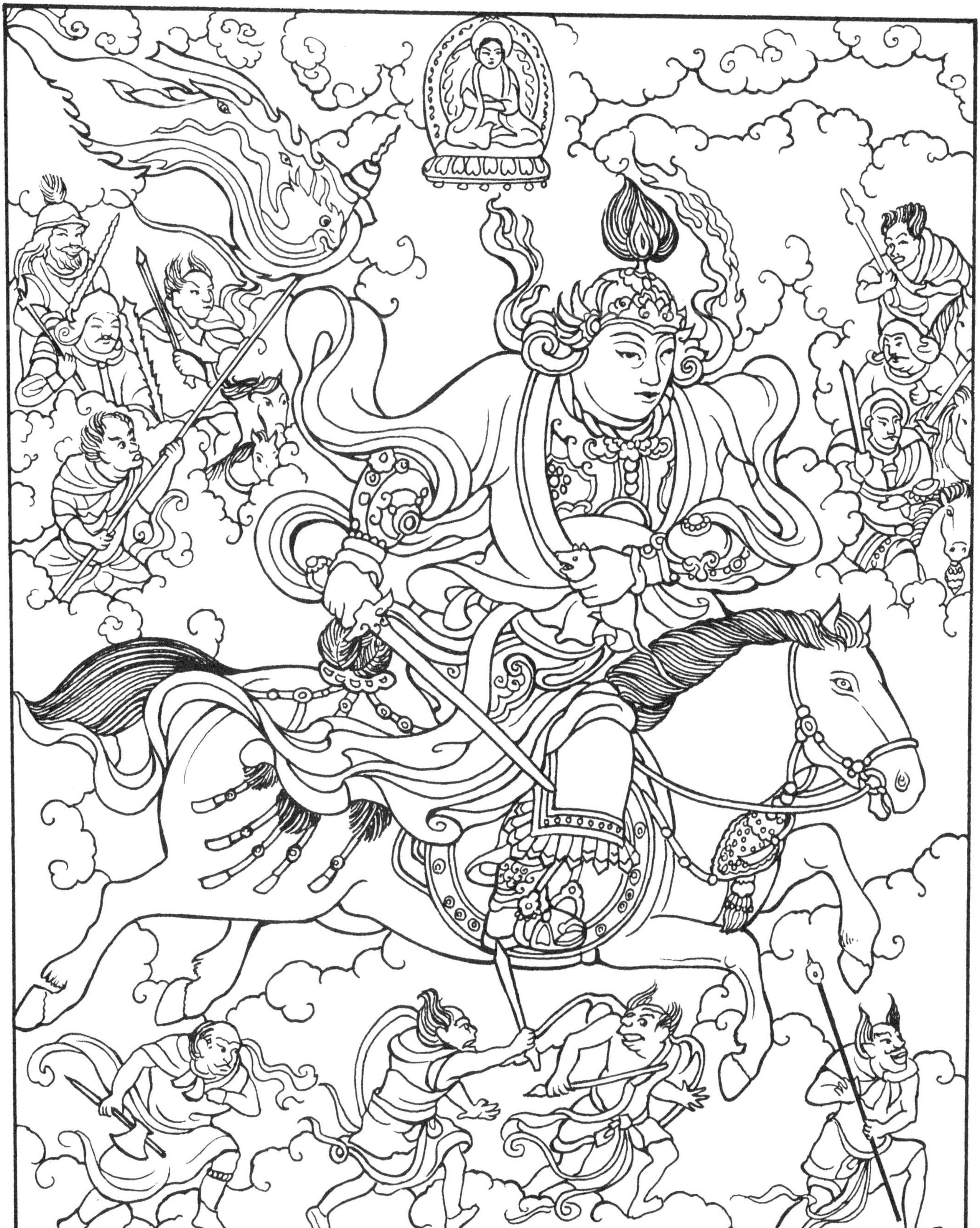

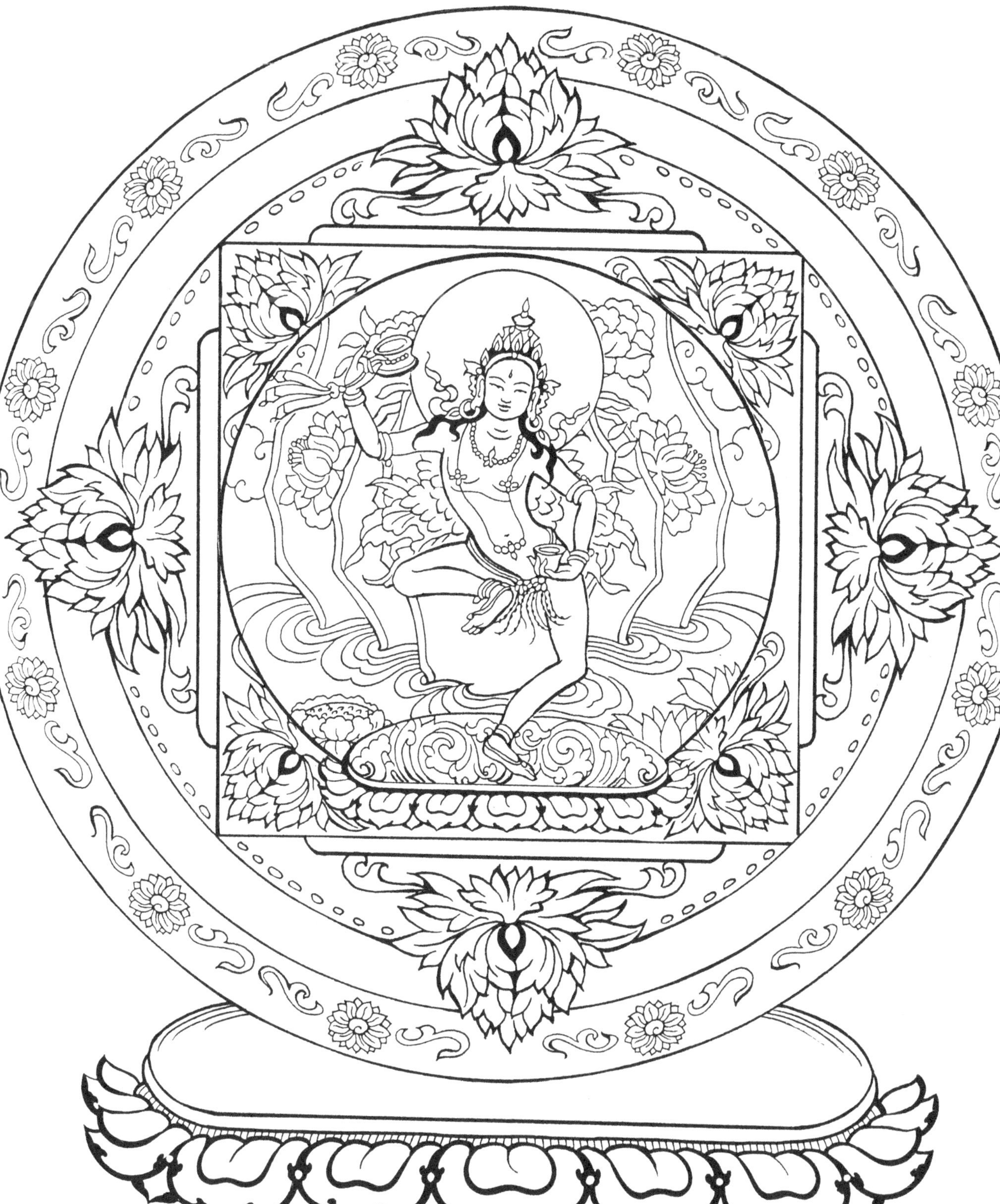

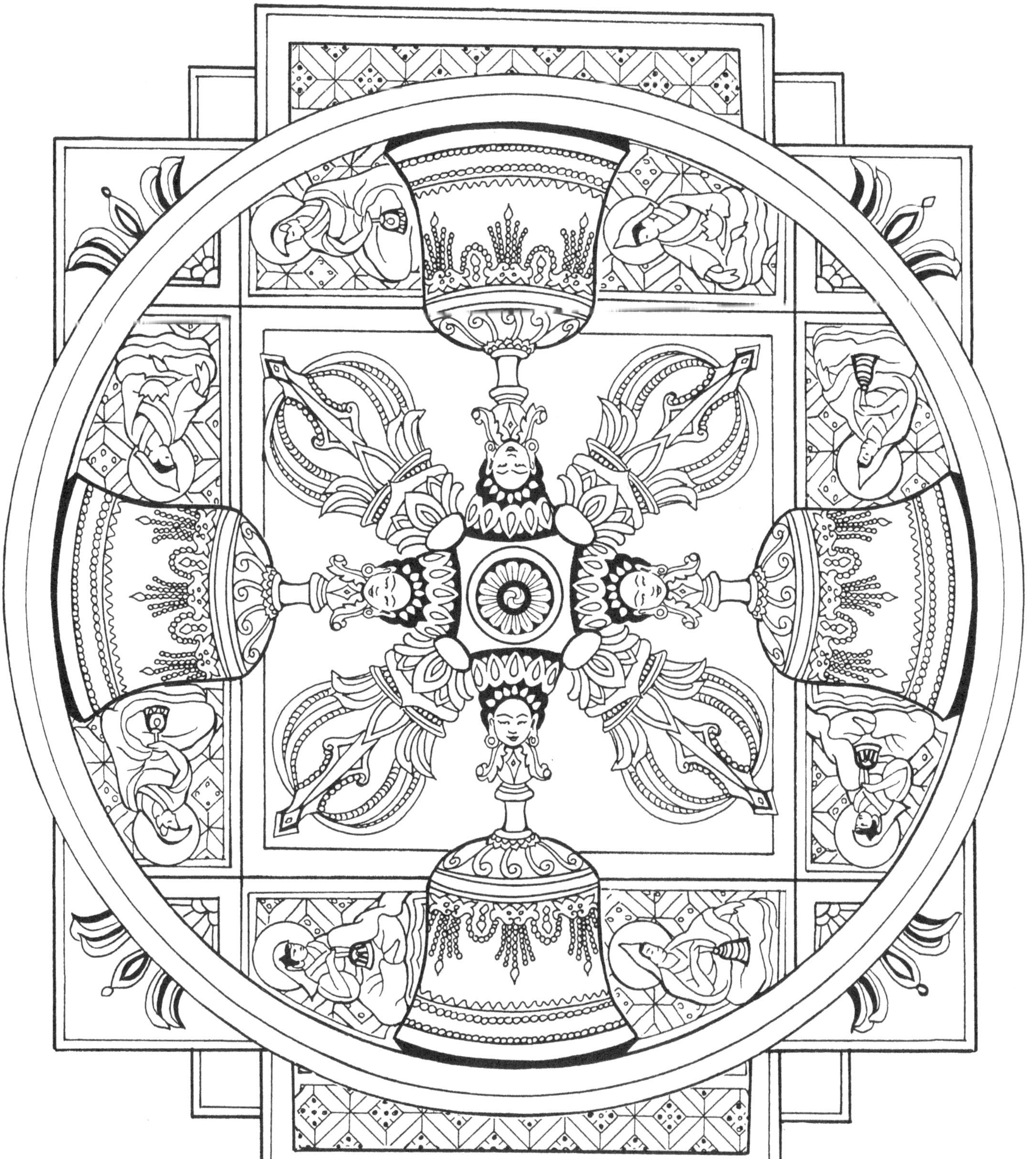

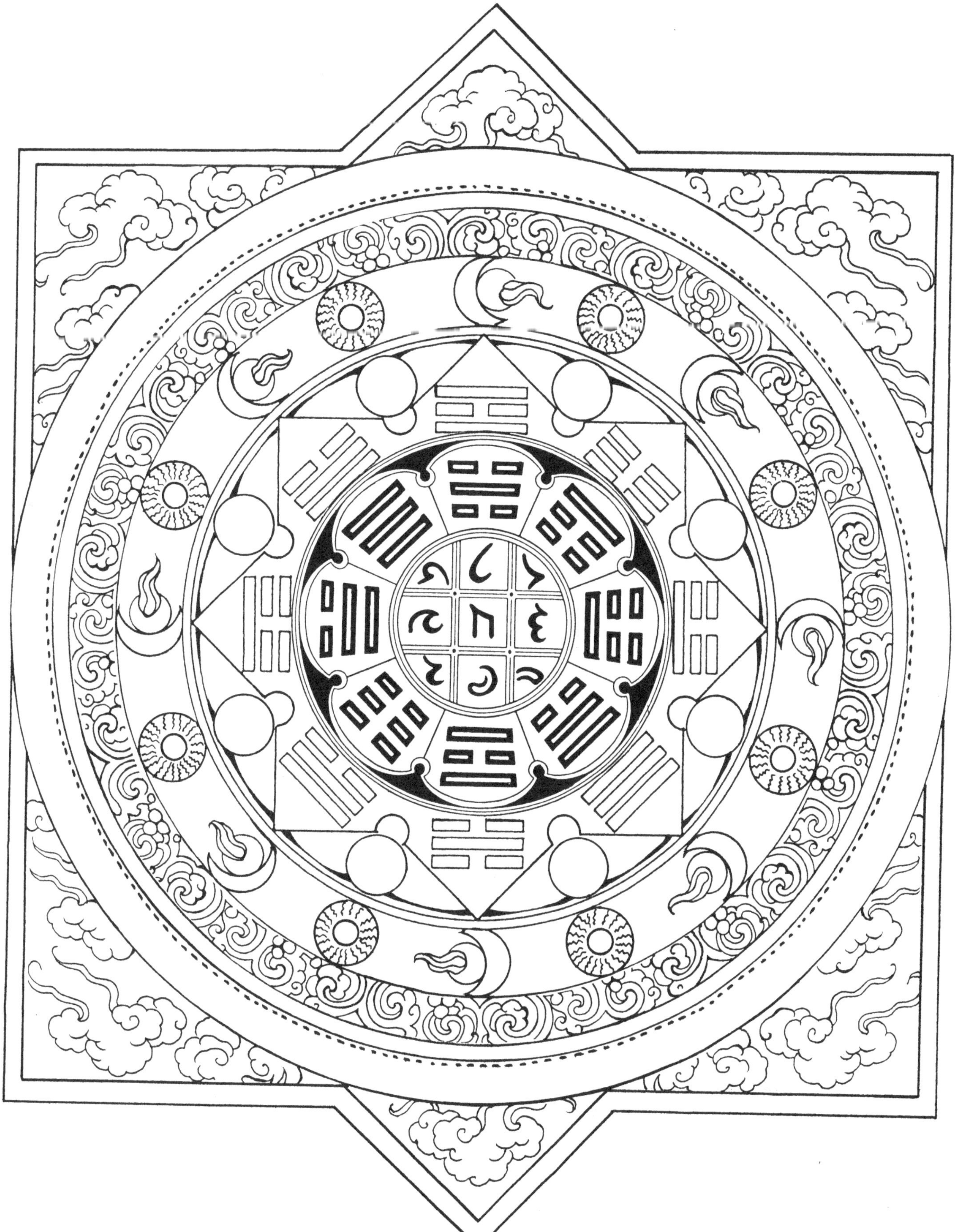

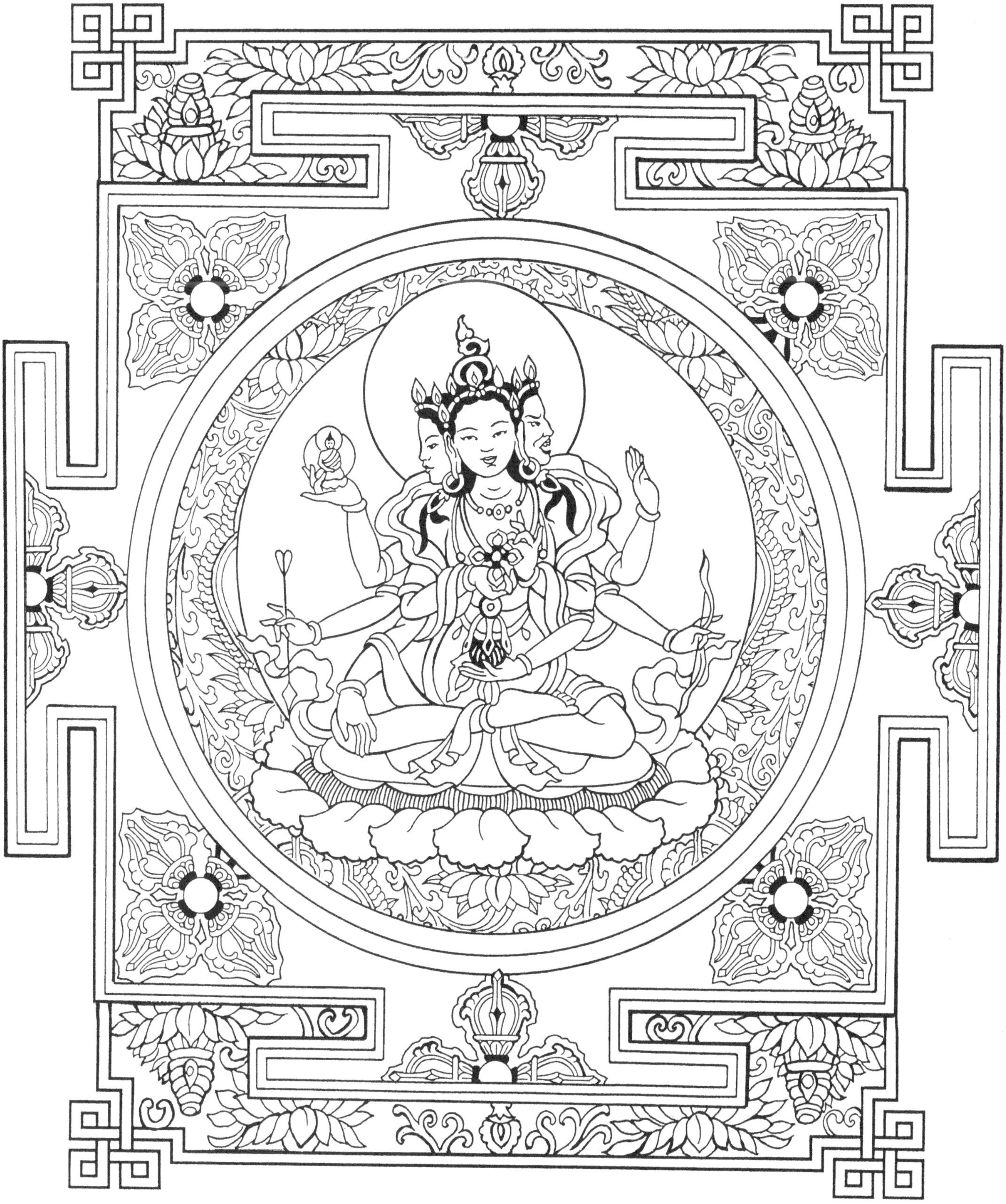

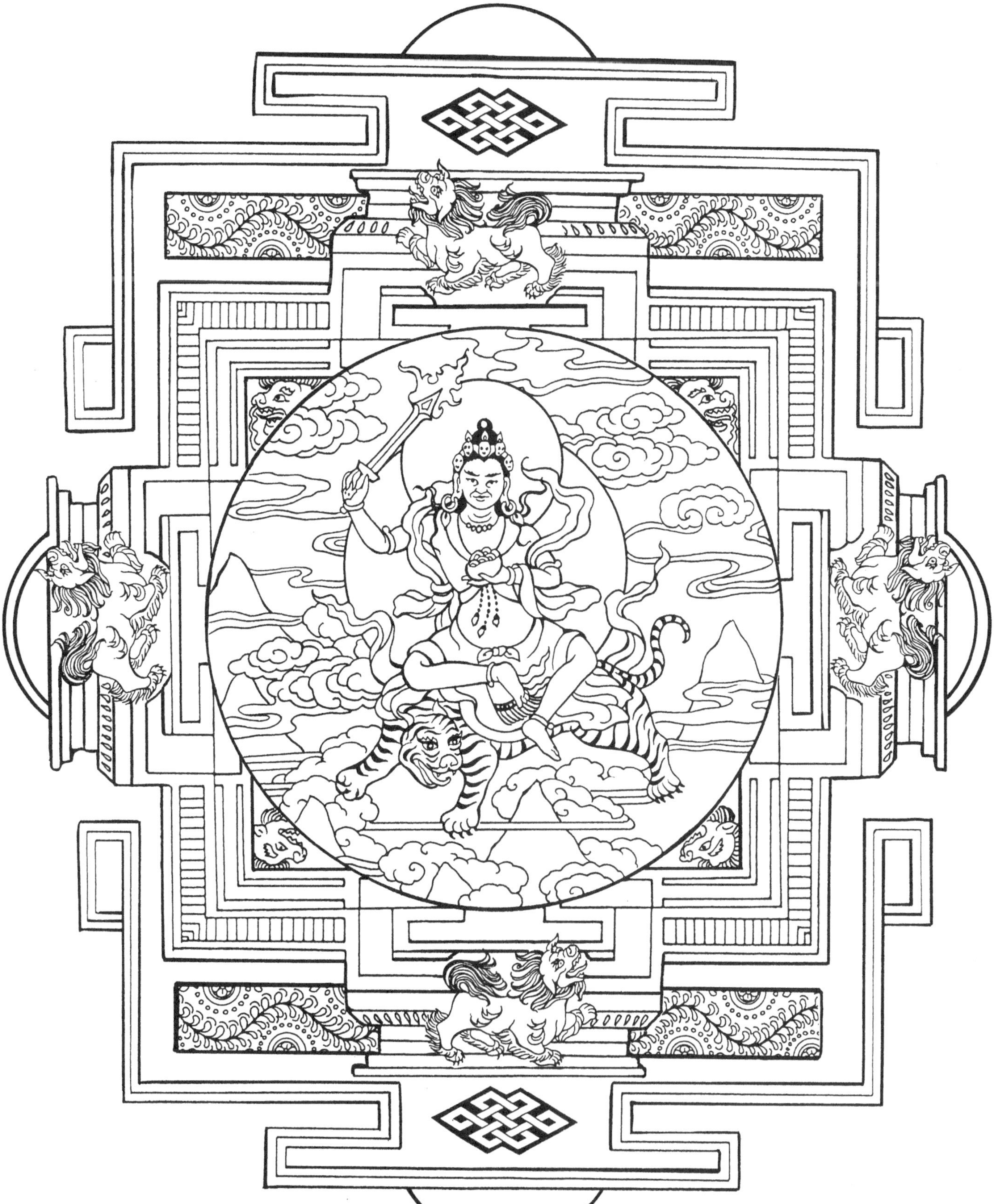

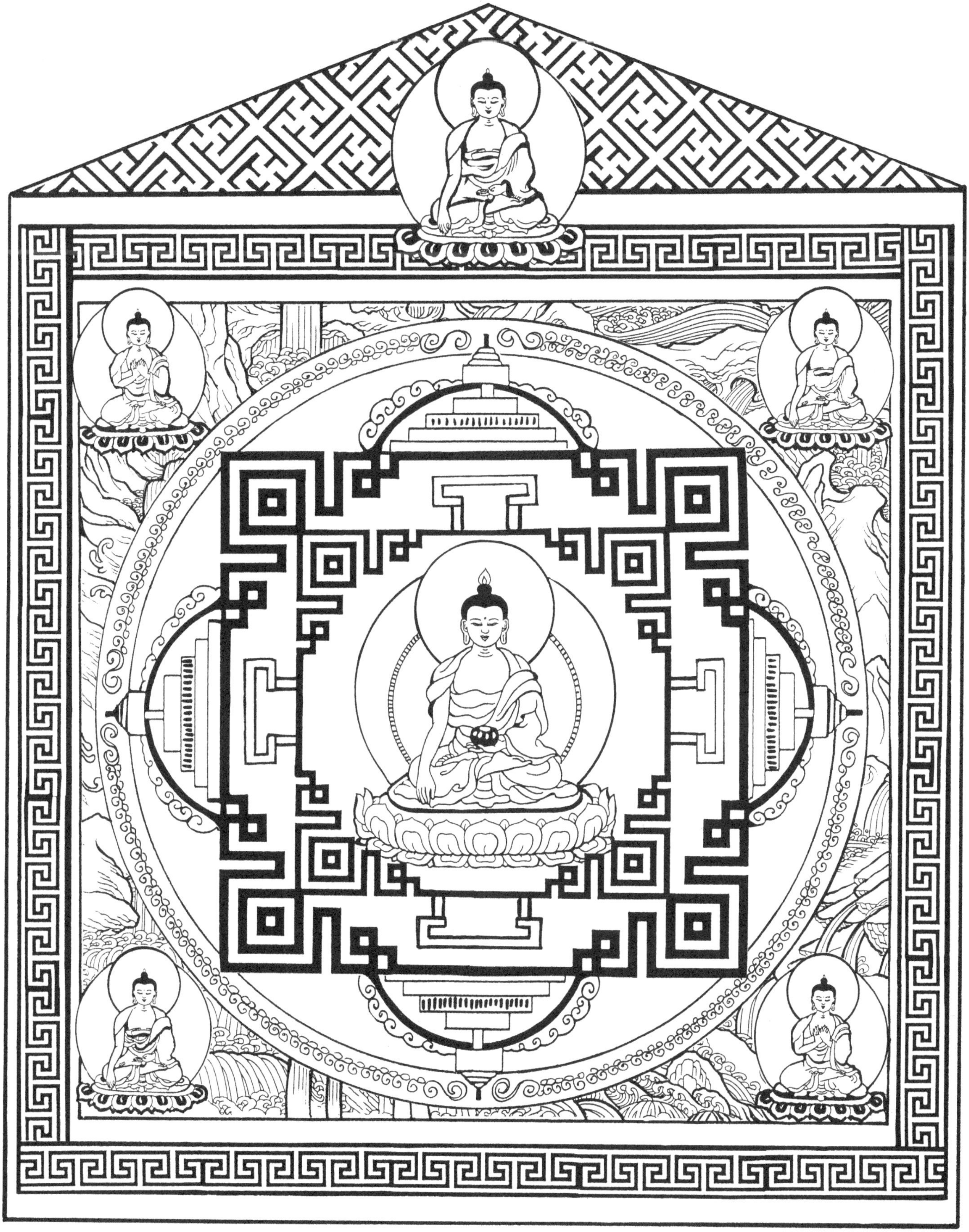

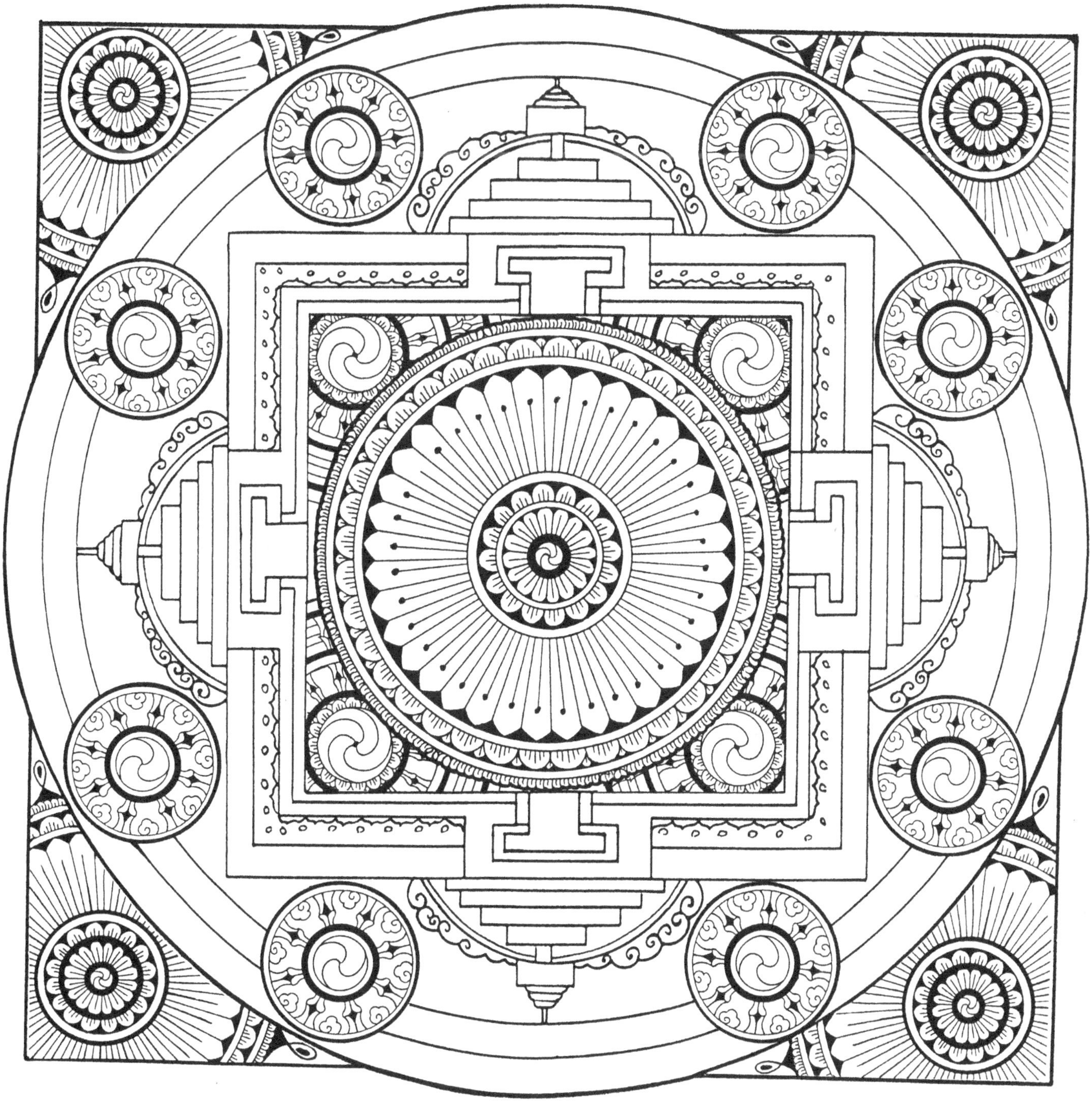

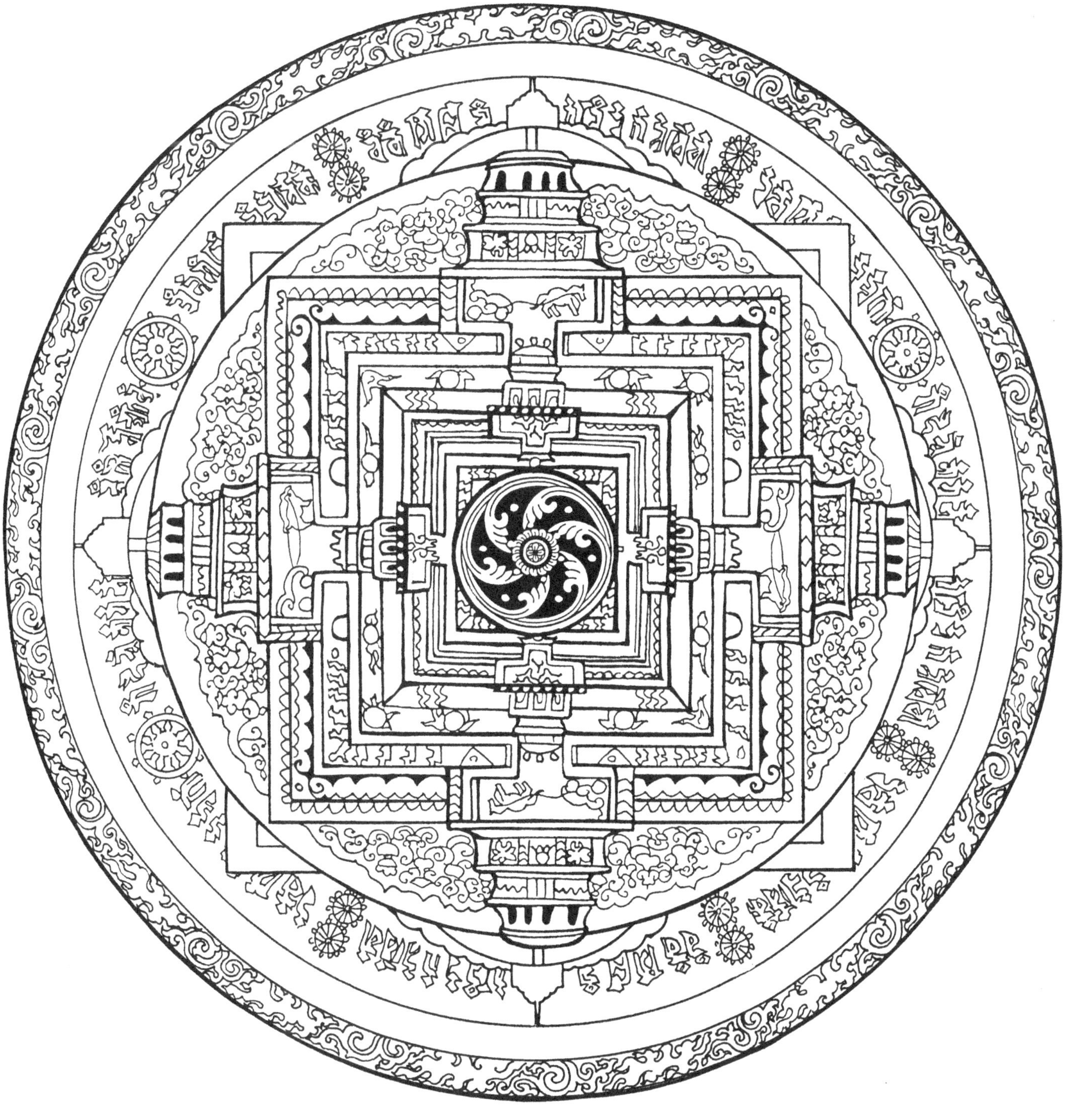

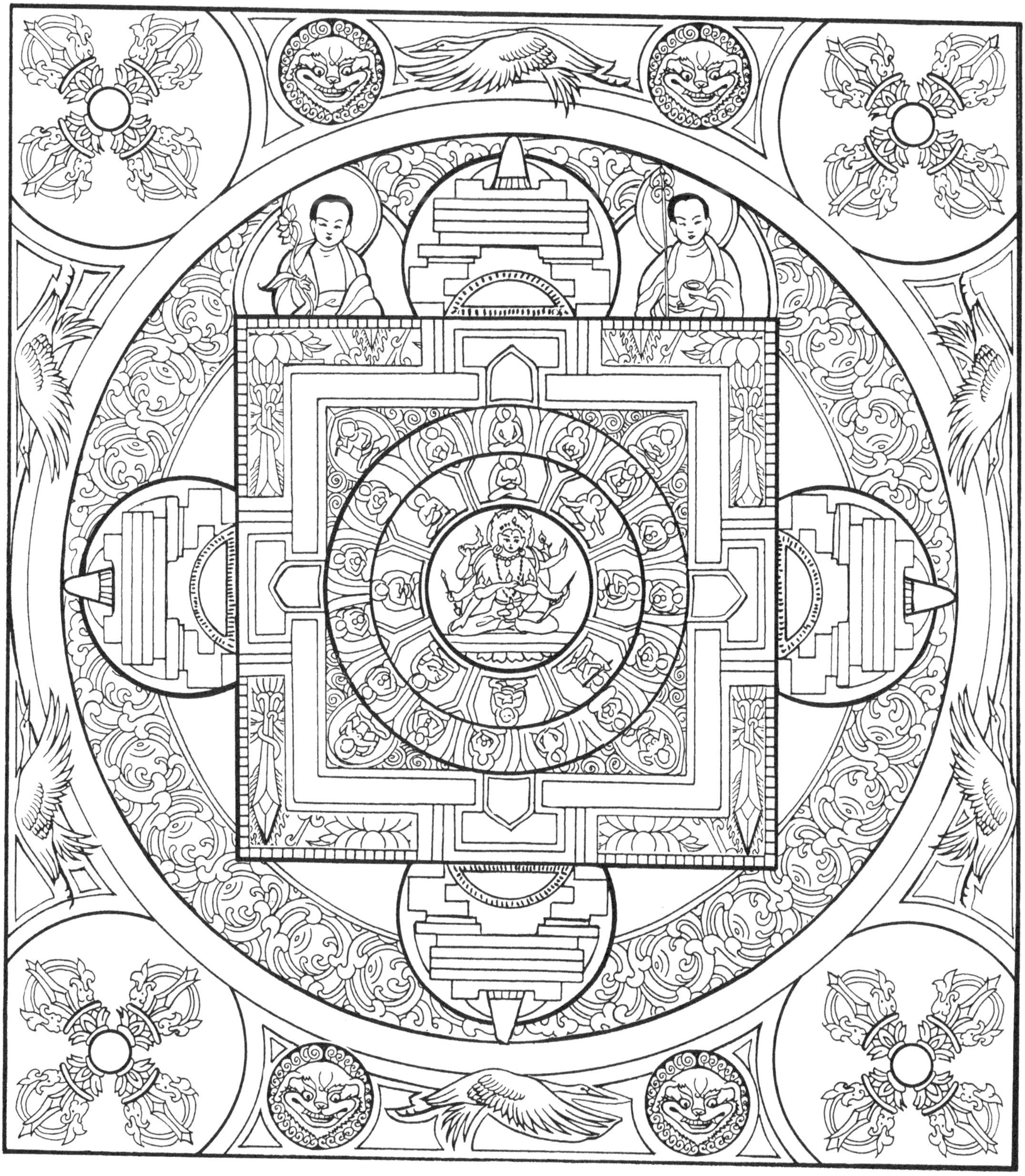

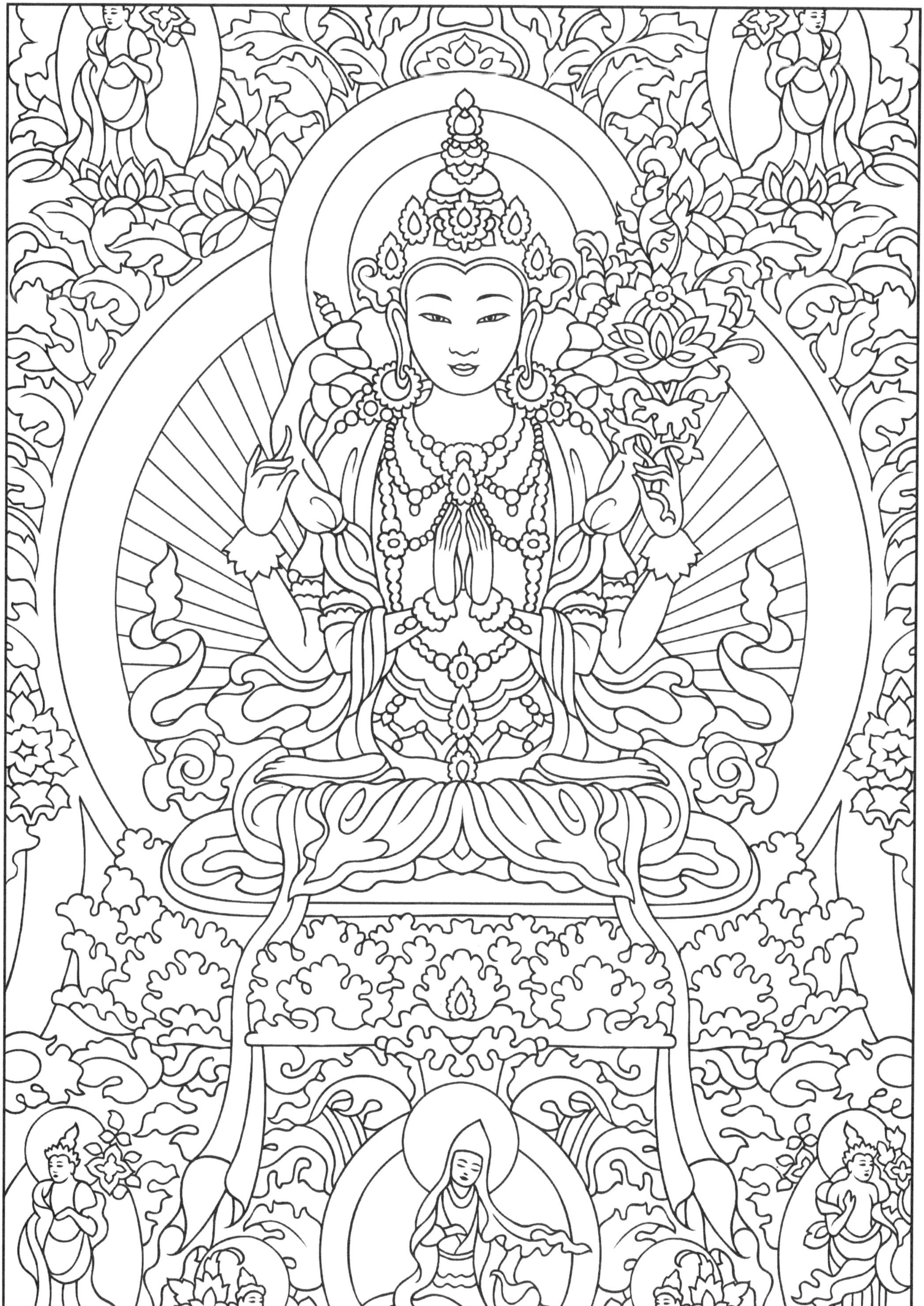